Cookbook t Linguine Lovers

Mouthwatering Pasta Dish Recipes to Satisfy Your Cravings

By

Angel Burns

© 2019 Angel Burns, All Rights Reserved.

License Notices

This book or parts thereof might not be reproduced in any format for personal or commercial use without the written permission of the author. Possession and distribution of this book by any means without said permission is prohibited by law.

All content is for entertainment purposes and the author accepts no responsibility for any damages, commercially or personally, caused by following the content.

Get Your Daily Deals Here!

Free books on me! Subscribe now to receive free and discounted books directly to your email. This means you will always have choices of your next book from the comfort of your own home and a reminder email will pop up a few days beforehand, so you never miss out! Every day, free books will make their way into your inbox and all you need to do is choose what you want.

What could be better than that?

Fill out the box below to get started on this amazing offer and start receiving your daily deals right away!

https://angel-burns.gr8.com

Table of Contents

Delicious Linguine Recipes 8

Chapter I - Seafood 9

    Recipe 1: Shrimp Scampi Linguine 10

    Recipe 2: Garlic Salmon Linguine 13

    Recipe 3: Linguine al Tonno 16

    Recipe 4: Clam Linguine.. 19

    Recipe 5: Seafood Medley with Linguine..................... 22

    Recipe 6: Crawfish Linguine.. 25

    Recipe 7: Sicilian-Style Mahi-Mahi Linguine 28

    Recipe 8: Creamy Catfish Alfredo 31

    Recipe 9: Lobster Linguine 35

    Recipe 10: Lemon Scallop Linguine............................. 39

Chapter II - Red Meat 42

    Recipe 11: Spanish Chorizo and Tomato Linguine 43

Recipe 12: Asian Pork Linguine 46

Recipe 13: Pounded Pork Parmesan with Linguine 49

Recipe 14: Bacon, Peach and Gorgonzola Linguine 52

Recipe 15: Picadillo Linguine 55

Recipe 16: Brie, Bacon, and Caramelized Onion Linguine 57

Recipe 17: Meatball Pasta in Cheesy Vodka Sauce 59

Recipe 18: Italian Sausage Linguine 62

Recipe 19: Linguine with Ham & Swiss Cheese 65

Recipe 20: Lamb Ragù with Linguine 68

Chapter III - Poultry 71

Recipe 21: Turkey Bacon Carbonara 72

Recipe 22: Chicken Linguine with Garlic Tomato Sauce 74

Recipe 23: Tequila Lime Chicken Linguine 77

Recipe 24: Chicken Stroganoff Linguine 81

Recipe 25: Spicy Turkey and Blue Cheese Linguine 84

Recipe 26: Italian Linguine Pesto with Chicken 87

Recipe 27: Pheasant Pesto Linguine 89

Recipe 28: Linguine with Duck Ragu 93

Recipe 29: Prosciutto, Lemon and Basil Linguine 96

Recipe 30: Linguine with Goose 99

Chapter IV - Meat-Free 102

Recipe 31: Super Cheesy Linguine 103

Recipe 32: Creamy Cajun Linguine 106

Recipe 33: Ricotta Linguini 109

Recipe 34: Greek-Style Linguine 111

Recipe 35: Pea and Basil Linguine 114

Recipe 36: Lemon, Feta, and Basil Linguine 118

Recipe 37: Linguine with Sun-Dried Tomatoes 121

Recipe 38: Ligurian Pasta Trenette 124

Recipe 39: Linguine with Mixed Nuts and Raisins 127

Recipe 40: Linguine Alla Puttanesca 130

About the Author 132

Author's Afterthoughts 134

Delicious Linguine Recipes

HHHHHHHHHHHHHHHHHHHHHHHHHHHHHHHH

Chapter I – Seafood

HHHHHHHHHHHHHHHHHHHHHHHHHHHHHHHHHH

Recipe 1: Shrimp Scampi Linguine

A seafood pasta dish that is as colorful as it is flavorsome and what's more, it's ready from pan to plate in less than half an hour.

Yield: 4

Preparation Time: 25mins

Ingredient List:

- 8 ounces linguine
- 3 tablespoons extra virgin olive oil (divided)
- 1 pound jumbo shrimp (peeled, deveined)
- 6 tablespoons unsalted butter
- 6 garlic cloves (peeled, minced)
- ¼ teaspoons dried crushed red pepper
- ¼ cup fresh parsley (coarsely chopped)
- 2 teaspoons lemon zest
- 1 tablespoon freshly squeezed lemon juice
- ¾ teaspoons salt

HHHHHHHHHHHHHHHHHHHHHHHHHHHHHHHHH

Instructions:

1. Cook the linguine according to the package instructions, until al dente. Drain.

2. Over moderate-high heat, heat 1 tablespoon of oil in a skillet.

3. Add half of the shrimp and cook for 60 seconds on each side, until opaque. Transfer to a plate, cover and keep the shrimp warm.

4. Repeat the process until all of the shrimp are cooked.

5. Over moderate heat, and in the same skillet, melt the butter.

6. Add the remaining oil, garlic, and red pepper and fry for a few minutes, until the garlic begins to brown.

7. Add the shrimp and stir to combine.

8. Finally, stir in the parsley followed by the lemon zest, fresh lemon juice, and salt.

9. Add the linguine and cook for 60 seconds to heat through while continually tossing to combine.

10. Serve at once, and enjoy.

Recipe 2: Garlic Salmon Linguine

Enjoy this surprisingly simple, yet super-tasty pasta dish made using canned salmon.

Yield: 6

Preparation Time:

Ingredient List:

- 16 ounce linguine
- ⅓ cup olive oil
- 3 cloves garlic (peeled, minced)
- 1 (15 ounce) can boneless, skinless salmon (drained)
- ¾ cup chicken broth
- ¼ cup fresh parsley (minced)
- ½ teaspoons sea salt
- ⅛ teaspoons cayenne pepper

HHHHHHHHHHHHHHHHHHHHHHHHHHHHHHHHH

Instructions:

1. Cook the linguine according to the package instructions. Drain and set to one side.

2. In the meantime, in a large pan, over moderate heat, heat the olive oil.

3. Add the garlic and cook while stirring until tender, for 60 seconds.

4. Add the salmon, broth, parsley, salt and cayenne pepper and stir until heated through.

5. Add the linguine to the pan, tossing to combine.

6. Serve.

Recipe 3: Linguine al Tonno

This midweek meal is as easy as opening a few cans!

Yield: 4

Preparation Time: 22mins

Ingredient List:

- 8 ounces linguine
- 2 (10¾ ounce) cans condensed cream of celery soup (undiluted)
- 1 cup 2% milk
- 1 teaspoon garlic powder
- ½ teaspoons seafood seasoning
- 3 (5 ounce) cans light water-packed tuna (drained, flaked)
- 1 (7½ ounce) jar marinated quartered artichoke hearts (drained)
- 2 medium tomatoes (chopped)
- 1 cup ripe black olives (pitted, sliced)

HHHHHHHHHHHHHHHHHHHHHHHHHHHHHHHHH

Instructions:

1. Cook the linguine according to package instructions. Drain and set to one side.

2. In the meantime, in a large pan, combine the celery soup with the milk, garlic powder, and seafood seasoning.

3. Stir in the flaked tuna followed by the artichokes, tomatoes, and olives. Bring the mixture to a boil. Turn the heat down to low.

4. Add the drained linguine to the pan, and gently stir to combine.

5. Serve.

Recipe 4: Clam Linguine

Linguine with clams in a creamy sauce is most probably one of the easiest meals you will ever make. It is the ideal appetizer to serve at a dinner party.

Yield: 8

Preparation Time: 35mins

Ingredient List:

- 1 pound linguine
- 1 medium onion (peeled, chopped)
- 2 tablespoons olive oil
- ¼ cup butter (cut into cubes)
- Four garlic cloves (peeled, minced)
- 3 tablespoons all-purpose flour
- 2 cups chicken broth
- 1 cup clam juice
- ½ cup heavy whipping cream
- 3 (6½ ounce) cans minced clams (drained)
- ½ cup fresh parsley (minced)
- ¼ teaspoons dried oregano
- ¼ teaspoons chipotle hot pepper sauce
- ⅛ teaspoons salt
- ⅛ teaspoons black pepper
- ⅛ teaspoons crushed red pepper flakes
- ⅔ cup grated Parmesan cheese (freshly grated)

HHHHHHHHHHHHHHHHHHHHHHHHHHHHHHHHH

Instructions:

1. Cook the linguine according to the package instructions, until al dente. Drain and put to one side.

2. In the meantime, in a pan, fry the onion in the oil and butter.

3. Add the garlic and fry for an additional 1-2 minutes.

4. Stir in the flour to incorporate, before gradually adding the chicken broth, clam juice and whipping cream.

5. Bring the mixture to boil and cook while stirring until thickened; this will take 2 minutes.

6. Add the clams along with the parsley, oregano, hot pepper sauce, salt, pepper, and red pepper flakes. Cook for 2-3 minutes until sufficiently heated through.

7. Add eh drained linguine to the pan followed by the grated cheese, and toss well to coat evenly.

8. Serve.

Recipe 5: Seafood Medley with Linguine

Scallops and shrimp come together to deliver an awesome pasta dish.

Yield: 8

Preparation Time: 40mins

Ingredient List:

- 1 large onion (peeled, chopped)
- 2 tablespoons butter
- 1 tablespoon olive oil
- 3 cloves garlic (peeled, minced)
- 1 cup white wine
- 2 (14 ounce) cans diced, fire-roasted tomatoes
- 1 tablespoon fresh rosemary (minced)
- 1 teaspoon sugar
- 1 teaspoon fresh oregano (minced)
- ¼ teaspoons salt
- ¼ teaspoons black pepper
- 16 ounces linguine
- 1 pound sea scallops
- 9 ounces raw shrimp (peeled, deveined)
- 2 tablespoons fresh parsley (minced)

HHHHHHHHHHHHHHHHHHHHHHHHHHHHHHHHH

Instructions:

1. In a large pan, sauté the onion in butter and olive oil until tender.

2. Add the garlic and cook for an additional 60 seconds.

3. Pour in the white wine and bring to boil, cooking until the liquid reduces to a yield of approximately ½ cup.

4. Add the tomatoes, rosemary, sugar, oregano, salt and black pepper.

5. Over moderate heat, bring to boil before reducing to a simmer and simmering uncovered for 15 minutes.

6. In the meantime, cook the linguine in boiling salted water until al dente.

7. Add the scallops along with the shrimp to the tomato mixture and cook until the shrimp turn pink and the scallops are opaque 4-5 minutes.

8. Fold in the parsley,

9. Drain the pasta and serve the seafood medley on top of the linguine.

Recipe 6: Crawfish Linguine

Whether you serve this as an appetizer or main, one thing's for sure, and that is, everyone will be coming back for more.

Yield: 2-4

Preparation Time: 25mins

Ingredient List:

- 8 ounces linguine
- 4 ounces butter
- ¼ cup olive oil
- 1 garlic clove (peeled, crushed)
- 3 ounces mushrooms (sliced)
- 1 pound crawfish tails
- 1 ¾ ounces green onions (chopped)
- 1 cup half and half cream
- 2 tablespoons Parmesan cheese (grated)
- 1 tablespoon fresh parsley (chopped)
- Salt and freshly ground black pepper

HHHHHHHHHHHHHHHHHHHHHHHHHHHHHHHH

Instructions:

1. Cook the linguine until al dente. Drain and set to one side.

2. In a skillet melt the butter along with the olive heat over moderate heat.

3. Add the garlic and mushrooms and sauté until fork tender.

4. Stir in the crawfish followed by the green onions. Turn the heat down to low and cook for an additional 5 minutes.

5. Pour in the half and half cream and stir to combine. Next, stir in the cheese and chopped parsley, and simmer for 5 minutes.

6. Season and serve over the al dente linguine.

Recipe 7: Sicilian-Style Mahi-Mahi Linguine

Mahi-mahi and any white wine are the perfect pairing, and this pasta dish is no exception. Did you know that mahi-mahi is Hawaiian for very strong?

Yield: 1-2

Preparation Time: 25mins

Ingredient List:

- 2 tablespoons olive oil
- 1 garlic clove (peeled)
- 10 cherry tomatoes (seeded, finely chopped)
- 7 ounces mahi-mahi (washed, patted dry, cut into small cubes)
- ½ glass Prosecco
- ½ teaspoons saffron
- 5 ounces whole grain linguine
- Sea salt
- 1 tablespoon Italian parsley (chopped)

HHHHHHHHHHHHHHHHHHHHHHHHHHHHHHHH

Instructions:

1. Fill a large pot, 2/3 of the way full with salted water, bring to boil. Add the linguine and cook until al dente. Drain and set to one side.

2. In a pan, warm the olive oil.

3. Add the garlic, and cook until lightly golden.

4. Add the tomatoes and sauté until fork tender, this will take 3-4 minutes. Remove and discard the garlic clove.

5. Add the cubes of fish and cook for a couple of minutes.

6. Pour in the Prosecco and simmer for 4 minutes, until cooked through. Stir in the saffron and season to taste.

7. Add the drained linguine to the sauce and garnish with parsley.

8. Serve.

Recipe 8: Creamy Catfish Alfredo

Catfish is mild, firm and protein rich. It is ideally suited to serve with pasta and a creamy sauce.

Yield: 8

Preparation Time: 50mins

Ingredient List:

- 12 ounces linguine
- 6 (4-6 ounce) farm-raised catfish fillets
- Paprika
- Sea salt and black pepper
- ¼ cup butter
- 2 tablespoons olive oil
- 1 medium onion (peeled, diced)
- 3 garlic cloves (peeled, minced)
- 1 red bell pepper (diced)
- ½ cup Romano cheese (grated)
- ½ pound mushrooms (diced)
- ½ cup cream
- ¼ teaspoons cayenne pepper
- 1 (14½ ounce) jar Alfredo sauce
- 2 cups fresh spinach (washed, torn into large pieces)
- ¼ cup Italian parsley (chopped)

HHHHHHHHHHHHHHHHHHHHHHHHHHHHHHHHH

Instructions:

1. Cook the linguine until al dente. Drain.

2. Lightly dust the catfish fillets with paprika and season with sea salt and black pepper.

3. Over moderate heat, in a pan, melt the butter and olive oil.

4. Add the onion, stirring until translucent and softened.

5. Add the garlic followed by the red pepper and mushroom and over moderate-high heat, cook until fork tender. Remove the mixture from the pan, using a slotted spoon,

6. Over moderate-high heat, heat the oil pan used to cook the veggies and mushrooms, you may need to add a drop more oil at this stage.

7. Add the fish to the pan and sear for a few minutes on each side until golden. Remove the fish from the pan and using kitchen paper towel, wipe the pan clean.

8. Return the veggies and mushrooms to the pan.

9. Pour in the jar of Alfredo sauce and add the cheese followed by the cream.

10. Bring to simmer, while continually stirring for 5 minutes, or until thickened.

11. Season with cayenne pepper, a pinch of salt and a dash of pepper.

12. Add the spinach to the pan,

13. Stir the drained pasta into the sauce.

14. Divide the linguine evenly between 8 pasta bowls and top each one with a fillet of fish.

15. Garnish with parsley and serve.

Recipe 9: Lobster Linguine

Lobster is a delicacy that is surprisingly simple to prepare at home but makes for an extremely impressive main course.

Yield: 6

Preparation Time: 40mins

Ingredient List:

- 1 cup vodka
- 1 cup water
- 4 (1¼ pound) lobsters
- Sea salt and black pepper
- 1 pound linguine
- 3 tablespoons olive oil
- 2 garlic cloves (peeled, very finely chopped)
- Crushed red pepper flakes
- 3 cups canned tomatoes (drained, coarsely chopped)
- 2 tablespoons fresh mint leaves (chopped)

HHHHHHHHHHHHHHHHHHHHHHHHHHHHHHHH

Instructions:

1. In a large pan, combine the vodka with the water, and bring to a simmer.

2. Add the lobsters and steam for between 8-10 minutes, until cooked through.

3. Allow to rest until cool.

4. Remove the tails along with the claws.

5. Halve the tails across their length, then halve once more crosswise.

6. Crack the lobster claws and set to one side. Discard the bodies and knuckles.

7. Cook the linguine according to the package instructions, until al dente.

8. In the meantime, in a pan over moderate heat, heat the oil.

9. Add the garlic and while stirring cook for a couple of minutes.

10. Stir in the red pepper flakes along with the canned tomatoes, and chopped mint. Simmer for a few minutes and season.

11. Drain the linguine and transfer to a serving platter.

12. Ladle the sauce over the linguine and top with the cooked lobster.

13. Serve.

Recipe 10: Lemon Scallop Linguine

Create a sophisticated pasta dish for two and serve with a glass of chilled Italian white wine.

Yield: 2

Preparation Time: 22mins

Ingredient List:

- 4 ounces linguine
- 1 teaspoon dried minced onion
- 3 tablespoons butter
- ¾ pound bay scallops
- 1/8 teaspoons lemon-pepper seasoning
- Dash of pepper
- 2 tablespoons freshly squeezed lemon juice
- Fresh parsley (minced)

HHHHHHHHHHHHHHHHHHHHHHHHHHHHHHHH

Instructions:

1. Cook the linguine, until al dente, according to the package instructions.

2. In the meantime, in a pan fry the onion in butter over moderate heat, until golden, 2-3 minutes.

3. Add the scallops along with the lemon-pepper seasoning. Add a dash of pepper and cook until the scallops are opaque and firm, this will take approximately 4-5 minutes.

4. Add the fresh lemon juice and cook for an additional 60 seconds.

5. Add the drained linguine to the pan and toss.

6. Garnish with parsley.

Chapter II – Red Meat

HHHHHHHHHHHHHHHHHHHHHHHHHHHHHHHHH

Recipe 11: Spanish Chorizo and Tomato Linguine

Linguine gets a Spanish makeover with spicy chorizo and red wine.

Yield: 4

Preparation Time: 30mins

Ingredient List:

- 5¼ ounces Spanish chorizo (casing removed, cut into cubes)
- Pinch fennel seeds
- 2 tablespoons olive oil
- 2 red onions (peeled, finely sliced)
- 2 garlic cloves (peeled, minced)
- 2 tablespoons tomato puree
- 2 teaspoons sugar
- Pinch dried chili flakes
- Small glass Spanish red wine
- 1 (14 ounce) can chopped tomatoes
- Sea salt and black pepper
- 1 pound linguine
- 1 teaspoon butter
- 3 ounces fresh spinach

HHHHHHHHHHHHHHHHHHHHHHHHHHHHHHHH

Instructions:

1. Heat a large frying pan and fry the cubes of chorizo along with the fennel seeds for 2-3 minutes, stirring until the sausage begins to release its spicy oil.

2. Add the olive oil, onions followed by the garlic and over low heat, stir for 3-4 minutes until softened.

3. Stir in the tomato purée together with the sugar, chilies and red wine.

4. Add the tomatoes, stir thoroughly and bring to a rolling simmer.

5. While the sauce bubbles, bring a large pan of water to the boil. Liberally season with a pinch of salt and cook the linguine in until al dente. Drain and return the linguine to the pot. Stir in the butter and toss to coat evenly.

6. Add the linguine to the tomato sauce, mixing until well coated.

7. Season.

8. Fold in the spinach and serve.

9. Taste and season. Stir in the spinach and serve

Recipe 12: Asian Pork Linguine

A sweet-spicy-salty sauce coats this al dente linguine and tender Asian pork pasta dish.

Yield: 4-6

Preparation Time: 20mins

Ingredient List:

- 6 ounces linguine
- ½ cup water
- 2 teaspoons cornstarch
- 2 tablespoons soy sauce
- ¼ cup smooth peanut butter
- ½ teaspoons powdered garlic
- 1 tablespoon honey
- Pinch powdered ginger
- 3 teaspoons sesame oil
- 1 pound boneless pork chops (chopped)
- 1 onion (peeled, sliced)
- 2 carrots (sliced)

HHHHHHHHHHHHHHHHHHHHHHHHHHHHHHHHH

Instructions:

1. Cook the linguine in boiling salted water until al dente. Drain and return to pot.

2. In the meantime, combine the water and cornstarch in a small bowl. Add the soy sauce, peanut butter, garlic, honey, and ginger stirring until combined.

3. Warm 2 teaspoons oil in a wok over moderate heat and add the pork, sauté until just cooked. Remove from the wok and keep warm. Add the onion and carrot to the wok, fry until softened.

4. Add the prepared sauce mixture to the wok, stir well and bring to a boil for a few minutes until it thickens.

5. Return the pork and pasta to the wok and toss well until combined.

Recipe 13: Pounded Pork Parmesan with Linguine

A filling dish for all the family to enjoy; it's filling, satisfying and super tasty.

Yield: 4

Preparation Time: 55mins

Ingredient List:

- 12 ounces linguine
- 2 tablespoons butter
- 4 (5 ounce) boneless center-cut pork chops
- ½ cup all-purpose flour
- ¼ teaspoons salt
- ¼ teaspoons pepper
- 1 large egg (lightly beaten)
- 1 cup Italian-seasoned breadcrumbs
- ½ cup olive oil
- 1 tablespoon fresh basil (chopped)
- 1 (26 ounce) jar tomato and basil pasta sauce
- 2 cups mozzarella cheese (shredded)
- ½ cup Parmesan cheese (grated)
- Fresh basil (chopped, to garnish)

HHHHHHHHHHHHHHHHHHHHHHHHHHHHHHHH

Instructions:

1. Cook the linguine in boiling salted water until al dente. Drain, toss with butter and set aside.

2. Arrange the pork on two sheets of kitchen wrap. Using a rolling pin, pound and flatten to no more than ¼" thickness.

3. In a bowl, combine the flour with the salt and black pepper.

4. Dredge the pork in the seasoned flour.

5. Next, dip the floured pork in the beaten egg before dredging in breadcrumbs.

6. In batches, fry the pork in a large pan over moderate-high heat in hot oil. Heat for a couple of minutes on each side until golden brown.

7. Arrange the pork in a single layer in a 13x9" casserole dish.

8. Stir 1 tablespoon of chopped basil into the pasta sauce.

9. Add the pasta sauce to the pork along with 2 cups of shredded mozzarella and grated Parmesan.

10. Bake in the oven at 400 degrees F or 20 minutes, or until the cheese is entirely melted and browned.

11. Serve with hot buttery linguine.

Recipe 14: Bacon, Peach and Gorgonzola Linguine

Light enough for lunch, yet sufficiently satisfying to be worthy of a main meal, this savory and sweet linguine is a real winner.

Yield: 4

Preparation Time: 30mins

Ingredient List:

- 12 ounces linguine
- 1 tablespoon olive oil
- 6 ounces bacon (chopped)
- 2 shallots (chopped)
- 1 peach (pitted, thinly sliced)
- ¾ cup Gorgonzola cheese (crumbled)
- 2 tablespoons fresh thyme

HHHHHHHHHHHHHHHHHHHHHHHHHHHHHHHHH

Instructions:

1. Cook the linguine according to the package instructions, until al dente. Drain and toss with olive oil.

2. In a frying pan, cook the bacon for 4-6 minutes, until crispy.

3. Remove the bacon from the pan and cook the shallots in the bacon fat for 2 minutes, until tender.

4. Add the slices of peach and cook until fork-tender, 3-4 minutes.

5. Return the linguine and bacon to the pan, tossing to incorporate.

6. Add the cheese and toss until combined.

7. Garnish with thyme and serve.

Recipe 15: Picadillo Linguine

A rich, meaty sauce with plump and juicy golden raisins is a deliciously comforting pasta dish.

Yield: 4

Preparation Time: 20mins

Ingredient List:

- 1 green bell pepper (seeded, chopped)
- 1 pound ground beef
- 2 garlic cloves (peeled, diced)
- 1 yellow onion (peeled, diced)
- ½ cup golden raisins
- 8 ounces jarred ragu pasta sauce
- 4 cups cooked linguine
- ½ cup fresh cilantro
- ½ cup queso fresco cheese (crumbled)

HHHHHHHHHHHHHHHHHHHHHHHHHHHHHHHH

Instructions:

1. Sauté the pepper, beef, garlic, and onion in a skillet for several minutes over moderately high heat.

2. Stir in the golden raisins and pasta sauce. Bring to a boil, turn the heat down and simmer for a few minutes until hot through.

3. Add the cooked pasta, cilantro and queso fresco toss well until combined.

Recipe 16: Brie, Bacon, and Caramelized Onion Linguine

Melt in the mouth brie, salty bacon, and sweet caramelized onions are an irresistible combination.

Yield: 2

Preparation Time: 30mins

Ingredient List:

- ¼ pound lean bacon (chopped)
- 2 garlic cloves (peeled, minced)
- 1 yellow onion (peeled, sliced)
- 1 tablespoon balsamic vinegar
- Salt
- ¼ cup whole milk
- 4 ounces rind-on brie (cut into cubes)
- 3 tablespoons Parmesan (grated)
- ½ pound cooked linguine

HHHHHHHHHHHHHHHHHHHHHHHHHHHHHHHH

Instructions:

1. Sauté the bacon in a skillet over moderately low heat. As the bacon browns, add the garlic and onion.

2. Over low heat, cook for 20 minutes until softened.

3. Add the vinegar and salt, cook for 60 seconds before adding the milk and cheeses. Stir until the cheeses melt.

4. Add the linguine and toss until it is coated evenly in the sauce.

5. Serve straight away.

Recipe 17: Meatball Pasta in Cheesy Vodka Sauce

Here's one for the grownups! This boozy meatball pasta dish is sure to be a big hit at your next dinner party or get-together.

Yield: 8

Preparation Time: 40mins

Ingredient List:

- Nonstick spray
- 2 tablespoons olive oil
- 2 teaspoons onion flakes
- 2 garlic cloves (peeled, minced)
- 4 cups jarred vodka pasta sauce
- ¼ teaspoons oregano
- 2½ pounds frozen meatballs (thawed)
- 8 cups cooked linguine
- 2 cups mozzarella cheese (grated)
- ½ cup Parmesan cheese (grated)

HHHHHHHHHHHHHHHHHHHHHHHHHHHHHHH

Instructions:

1. Preheat the main oven to 350 degrees F. Spritz a glass baking dish with nonstick spray. Set to one side.

2. Warm the olive oil in a skillet over moderate heat, add the onion and garlic, sauté for a couple of minutes before stirring in the pasta sauce and oregano, cook for 5-6 minutes until hot through.

3. Add the meatballs, bring the mixture to a simmer for several minutes until the meatballs are hot through.

4. Add the cooked pasta and mozzarella, toss well until combined.

5. Transfer the mixture to the baking dish. Sprinkle with Parmesan and bake in the oven for just over 20 minutes until bubbling.

6. Serve straight away.

Recipe 18: Italian Sausage Linguine

This easy sausage linguine is the perfect dish to celebrate National Linguine Day.

Yield: 4

Preparation Time: 25mins

Ingredient List:

- ½ teaspoons olive oil
- 6½ ounces Italian sausage (casing removed)
- 2 garlic cloves (peeled, crushed)
- ½ tablespoons oregano
- 16 ounces passata
- Dash of pepper
- 9 ounces linguine pasta
- 3¼ tablespoons sour cream
- Basil leaves (to serve)

HHHHHHHHHHHHHHHHHHHHHHHHHHHHHHHHHH

Instructions:

1. Bring a large pan of salted water to boil.

2. To a frying pan, add ½ teaspoon of olive oil.

3. Add the sausage meat, while breaking it up, using the back of a wooden spoon, and brown.

4. Add the garlic along with the oregano and fry for 30 seconds.

5. Add the passata to the pan and season with a dash of pepper, cook for 5 minutes to reduce.

6. Add the linguine to the boiling salted water and cook until al dente.

7. Turn off the heat and add the sour cream, stirring to incorporate entirely.

8. Return to low heat, taste and season.

9. Toss the linguine in the sauce to coat and garnish with basil leaves.

Recipe 19: Linguine with Ham & Swiss Cheese

Discover this quick and easy recipe with al dente linguine, Swiss cheese, and deli ham. Delicious!

Yield: 8

Preparation Time: 1hour 20mins

Ingredient List:

- 8 ounces linguine (snapped in half)
- 2 cups cooked ham (cut into cubes)
- 1 (10¾ ounce) can condensed cream of mushroom soup, undiluted
- 2½ cups Swiss cheese (shredded, divided)
- 1 cup sour cream
- 1 medium onion (peeled, chopped)
- ½ cup green pepper (finely chopped)
- 2 tablespoons butter (melted)

HHHHHHHHHHHHHHHHHHHHHHHHHHHHHHHH

Instructions:

1. Cook the linguine in boiling salted water until al dente. Drain.

2. In the meantime, in a bowl combine the ham with the soup, 2 cups of cheese, sour cream, onion, pepper, and butter.

3. Add the linguine, tossing to coat evenly.

4. Transfer the mixture to a greased 13x9: casserole dish, cover with a lid and bake at 350 degrees F, for 35 minutes.

5. Remove the lid and scatter with the remaining cheese.

6. Bake in the oven for an additional 15-20 minutes, until the cheese is entirely melted.

Recipe 20: Lamb Ragù with Linguine

In Italian cooking, a ragu is typically a meat-based sauce that is generally served with pasta; it was created in the 18th century by Alberto Alvisi.

Yield: 4-6

Preparation Time: 25mins

Ingredient List:

- 1 tablespoon sunflower oil
- 1 onion (peeled, finely chopped)
- 1 clove garlic, peeled and crushed
- 7 ounces Shiraz
- 1 (14 ounce) can Italian chopped tomatoes
- 2 ounces black olives (pitted, chopped)
- 1 tablespoon sundried tomato paste
- 2 teaspoons dried oregano
- Pinch crushed chilies
- 14 ounces leftover roast lamb (chopped small)
- 1 pound fresh linguine

HHHHHHHHHHHHHHHHHHHHHHHHHHHHHHHH

Instructions:

1. In a pan, heat the oil. Add the onion and cook for 5 minutes.

2. Add the garlic and Shiraz wine and boil for a few minutes.

3. Stir in the tomatoes, black olives, tomato paste, oregano, chilies, and lamb.

4. Bring to boil, before reducing to a simmer and cooking until reduced, for 15 minutes. Season with a dash of black pepper.

5. In the meantime, cook the linguine in boiling salted water for 1-3 minutes, drain.

6. Divide the linguine between pasta bowls and top with the lamb ragu.

7. Enjoy.

Chapter III – Poultry

HHHHHHHHHHHHHHHHHHHHHHHHHHHHHHHHHH

Recipe 21: Turkey Bacon Carbonara

Everyone loves a creamy carbonara, what you may be surprised to learn is that this recipe using turkey bacon comes in at less than 300 calories per serving.

Yield: 6

Preparation Time: 35mins

Ingredient List:

- Nonstick cooking spray
- 8 slices turkey bacon
- 1 cup Parmesan cheese (freshly grated)
- 1-pint refrigerated egg product
- 8 ounces linguine
- ¼ cup green onions (chopped)

Instructions:

1. Spritz a 9" square casserole dish with nonstick spray.

2. In a bowl, combine the bacon with the cheese and egg product.

3. Cook the linguine in boiling salted water, until al dente. Drain.

4. Add the hot linguine and green onions to the bacon mixture, stirring to coat evenly. Transfer to the casserole dish and cover loosely with plastic wrap.

5. On moderate-high, microwave the carbonara for approximately 8-12 minutes, until the eggs are set.

6. Allow to stand for 5 minutes, before serving.

Recipe 22: Chicken Linguine with Garlic Tomato Sauce

Tender chicken in a garlic and tomato sauce served over al dente linguine makes a super supper or delicious dinner from pot to plate in just half an hour.

Yield: 2

Preparation Time: 30mins

Ingredient List:

- Olive oil
- ½ onion (peeled, diced small)
- 1 garlic clove (peeled, diced)
- 7 ounces canned tomatoes
- 7 ounces chicken breast
- 5 ounces linguine
- Salt and black pepper
- Parmesan cheese (freshly grated)

HHHHHHHHHHHHHHHHHHHHHHHHHHHHHHHHH

Instructions:

1. Add a drop of oil to a pan and over high heat, cook the onion and garlic until just browned.

2. Add the tomatoes and reduce the heat to moderate. Simmer for 15 minutes, while breaking down the tomatoes using the back of a wooden spoon.

3. While the sauce simmers, fry the chicken in a drop of olive oil, until browned all over and cooked through so that the chicken's juices run clear.

4. Cook the linguine until al dente.

5. Add the browned chicken to the tomato mixture and continue simmering.

6. Drain the pasta and add it to the mixture. Season to taste and stir to combine.

7. Garnish with Parmesan.

8. Serve.

Recipe 23: Tequila Lime Chicken Linguine

Tequila and lime are a marriage made in heaven but combined with juicy chicken and heavy cream; they are sublime.

Yield: 4-6

Preparation Time: 25mins

Ingredient List:

- 1 pound chicken (cut into bite-sized pieces)
- ¼ cup soy sauce
- 4 tablespoons butter (divided)
- 6 tablespoons garlic (peeled, crushed)
- 2 tablespoons jalapeno (minced)
- ½ cup fresh cilantro (chopped)
- ½ cup chicken stock
- 2 tablespoons freshly squeezed lime juice
- 2 tablespoons silver tequila
- 1 pound linguine
- 3 bell peppers (1 red, 1 orange, 1 green, finely sliced¬)
- 1 small red onion (peeled, finely sliced)
- 1½ cups heavy cream
- Chopped cilantro (to garnish)

HHHHHHHHHHHHHHHHHHHHHHHHHHHHHHHH

Instructions:

1. Add the chicken to a bowl. Pour the soy sauce over the chicken and put to one side to marinate.

2. In the meantime, prepare the remaining ingredients.

3. In a pan, over moderate heat, melt half of the butter. Add the garlic along with the jalapeno, cilantro, stock, fresh lime juice, and tequila. Turn the heat up to high, and bring to boil.

4. Simmer, until the mixture reduces by 50 percent, this will take around 5 minutes.

5. Take the pan off the heat and set to one side.

6. Over moderate to high heat, in a skillet melt the remaining butter. Add the chicken and sear for 2-3 minutes, to allow the chicken meat to become white in color.

7. In the meantime, cook the linguine according to the package instructions, until al dente. Drain.

8. Add the red, orange and green bell peppers along with the red onion to the chicken and fry until the veggies are tender yet crisp 5-7 minutes.

9. Add the tequila sauce, stirring to incorporate.

10. Add the cooked linguine and heavy cream.

11. Turn the heat off and toss the ingredients to combine.

12. Garnish with chopped cilantro and serve.

Recipe 24: Chicken Stroganoff Linguine

This creamy chicken linguine is sure to become a firm family favorite and have everyone rushing to get home.

Yield: 4

Preparation Time: 55mins

Ingredient List:

- 10 ounces linguine
- Olive oil
- Sea salt and black pepper
- 3-4 skinless chicken breasts
- 2 teaspoons garlic (peeled, crushed)
- 2 tablespoons unsalted butter
- ½ cup baby Bella mushrooms (thinly sliced)
- ¼ cup sliced Vidalia onion (peeled, sliced)
- 2½ tablespoons all-purpose flour
- 2 cups chicken broth
- 2 tablespoons Worcestershire sauce
- ⅓ cup sour cream

HHHHHHHHHHHHHHHHHHHHHHHHHHHHHHHH

Instructions:

1. Cook the linguine in boiling salted water, until al dente. Drain, and put to one side.

2. Preheat 2 tablespoons of olive oil in a grill pan.

3. Season the chicken and grill for 10-15 minutes each side, until the chicken's juices run clear. Set aside to rest for 5 minutes, before slicing. Set to one side.

4. In frying pan over moderate heat, add 2 tablespoons of olive oil followed by the garlic and unsalted butter. When the butter is entirely melted, add the mushrooms along with the onions and cook until fork tender.

5. Add the flour, stirring to combine.

6. Pour in the broth and add the Worcestershire sauce. Increase the heat to high and continually stir. Once boiling, reduce the heat to moderate and add the sliced chicken. Gently stirring until combined, cook for an additional 5-7 minutes.

7. Turn off the heat and gently fold in the cream.

8. Serve the chicken stroganoff over the cooked linguine and enjoy.

Recipe 25: Spicy Turkey and Blue Cheese Linguine

Blue cheese can add a new dimension to an already flavorsome pasta dish, and by adding a dash or two of hot sauce, you will certainly spice things up a little.

Yield: 4-6

Preparation Time:

Ingredient List:

- 8 ounces linguine
- 2 tablespoons butter
- 1 cup onion (peeled, chopped)
- 1 cup celery (chopped)
- ¾ cup carrots (chopped)
- 1 teaspoon garlic (peeled, minced)
- 1 tablespoon all-purpose flour
- ½ teaspoons salt
- 2 cups whole milk
- 4 ounces cream cheese (softened)
- 4 cooked, roasted turkey breast tenderloins (chopped)
- 2 -3 tablespoons Louisiana hot sauce (to taste)
- ¼ cup blue cheese (crumbled)

HHHHHHHHHHHHHHHHHHHHHHHHHHHHHHHH

Instructions:

1. Cook the linguine according to package instructions, until al dente. Drain.

2. In the meantime, to a large pan, add the butter, sauté the onion along with the celery, carrot, and garlic until fork tender.

3. Stir in the flour and salt until combined before gradually pouring in the milk.

4. Bring to boil and cook while stirring for between 1-2 minutes, until the sauce has slightly thickened.

5. Add the cream cheese and stir until entirely melted.

6. Add the chopped turkey. Stir in 2 tablespoons of hot sauce, taste and add more if needed.

7. Cook, while stirring until heated through.

8. Add the drained linguine to the pan and toss evenly to coat in the sauce.

9. Garnish with crumbled blue cheese and serve.

Recipe 26: Italian Linguine Pesto with Chicken

Very little washing-up to do when you prepare this simple dish which makes it ideal for those days when there isn't even time to breathe!

Yield: 4

Preparation Time: 15mins

Ingredient List:

- 8 ounces linguine
- 6 ounces ready-to-use grilled Italian chicken strips
- 1 cup mature Cheddar cheese (shredded)
- ¾ cup frozen corn (thawed)
- 1 (3½ ounce) jar store-bought pesto
- ¼ cup seasoned breadcrumbs
- ¼ teaspoons crushed red pepper flakes
- ¼ teaspoons black pepper

НННННННННННННННННННННННННННННННННН

Instructions:

1. Cook the linguine in boiling salted water until al dente. Drain and set to one side.

2. Add the chicken strips along with the Cheddar cheese, corn, pesto, breadcrumbs, pepper flakes and black pepper, gently stir to coat evenly.

3. Add the chicken mixture to the drained linguine and toss to combine.

4. Serve.

Recipe 27: Pheasant Pesto Linguine

If you are looking for an alternative way to prepare pheasant, then look no further than this rich dish. Enjoy rich pheasant breasts cooked in white wine, served on a bed of creamy pesto linguine.

Yield: 4

Preparation Time: 1hour 30mins

Ingredient List:

- 4 skinless, pheasant breast halves
- ¾ cup white wine
- 8 ounces linguine
- 1 tablespoon olive oil
- ½ onion (peeled, chopped)
- 8 mushrooms (sliced)
- 1 cup fresh spinach leaves (chopped)
- ½ cup white wine
- ¼ cup heavy cream
- ¼ cup pesto sauce
- 2 tablespoons Parmesan cheese (grated)

HHHHHHHHHHHHHHHHHHHHHHHHHHHHHHHHH

Instructions:

1. Preheat the main oven to 350 degrees F.

2. Arrange the pheasant breasts in a casserole dish, and pour in the white wine.

3. Bake in the oven for 40-45 minutes, until the pheasant is no longer pink in the center. A thermometer inserted into the bird, near the bones, should register 165 degrees F.

4. Remove from the oven and set aside to cool.

5. Once cool, remove the meat from the bones and cut into bite-size pieces.

6. Cook the pasta in boiling salted water until al dente. Drain and set to one side.

7. In the meantime, heat the oil over moderate heat in a frying pan or skillet.

8. Add the onions and stir until translucent and softened, for 4-5 minutes.

9. Add the mushrooms along with the spinach, and pheasant.

10. Cook until the mushrooms are beginning to soften.

11. Pour in the white wine, cover with a lid and cook for 5 minutes.

12. Stir in the heavy cream followed by the pesto sauce.

13. Take off the heat.

14. Transfer the linguine to a bowl, pour the pheasant sauce over the top of the linguine and garnish with Parmesan.

15. Serve.

Recipe 28: Linguine with Duck Ragu

Roasted duck breast teams with al dente linguine to create a restaurant-worthy main course or appetizer.

Yield: 4

Preparation Time: 22mins

Ingredient List:

- 2 duck breast fillets (trimmed)
- Salt and freshly ground black pepper

Sauce:

- 2 tablespoons sunflower oil
- 1 onion (peeled, finely chopped)
- 2 celery sticks (trimmed, chopped)
- 3 cloves garlic, peeled and crushed
- 1 (14 ounce) can chopped tomatoes
- 12 ounces fresh linguine
- 1 tablespoon fresh oregano (torn)

Instructions:

1. Season the duck with salt and pepper all over.

2. Add the duck, skin side facing downwards, to a nonstick saucepan, over high heat and cook until the skin is golden and the duck releases its fat.

3. Flip over and cook the other side until crispy. Remove from the heat and set aside to rest.

4. In the meantime, prepare the sauce. In a pan heat the sunflower oil. When hot, add the onion, celery, and garlic and over low heat, fry until softened but not yet browned.

5. Add the tomatoes, stirring well to combine and season. Gently cook in order to reduce the sauce slightly.

6. Add the linguine to a pan of boiling salted water and cook until al dente, for 1-3 minutes. Drain.

7. Add the drained pasta to the sauce, stirring to coat evenly.

8. Shred the cooked duck and transfer to the sauce.

9. Garnish with oregano and serve.

Recipe 29: Prosciutto, Lemon and Basil Linguine

A fresh tasting dish that is ideal as a lite lunch or early evening meal.

Yield: 6

Preparation Time: 20mins

Ingredient List:

- 14 ounces linguine
- 1 tablespoon olive oil
- 2 ounces prosciutto (torn into bite-sized pieces)
- Freshly squeezed juice of 1 lemon
- 2 medium egg yolks
- 3 tablespoons crème fraiche
- A handful of basil leaves
- Parmesan cheese (grated)

HHHHHHHHHHHHHHHHHHHHHHHHHHHHHHHHH

Instructions:

1. Cook the linguine in boiling salted water, until al dente.

2. In a pan, heat the olive oil, add the torn prosciutto and fry until crisp and golden.

3. Drain the linguine, and reserve ½ cup of the pasta cooking water.

4. Return the linguine to the pan.

5. Add the ham to the pasta.

6. In a bowl, combine the fresh lemon juice with the egg yolks, and crème fraiche and add to the pan together with the basil and Parmesan cheese. Using tongs, mix to combine, adding a drop of the pasta cooking water, if necessary.

7. Serve, garnished with Parmesan cheese.

Recipe 30: Linguine with Goose

A rich and satisfying dish seasoned with herbs is a show-stopping entrée for any important occasion.

Yield: 6-8

Preparation Time: 1hour 10mins

Ingredient List:

- ⅓ cup olive oil (divided)
- 10 ounces skinless, boneless goose breast (minced)
- 6 ounces goose liver (minced)
- 1½ tablespoons sage (minced)
- 2 tablespoons rosemary (minced)
- 2 celery stalks (minced)
- 1 teaspoon red chili flakes (crushed)
- 1 yellow onion (peeled, minced)
- 1 carrot (peeled, minced)
- 1 cup dry white wine
- 2 (14 ounce) cans whole peeled tomatoes, crushed
- Sea salt and black pepper
- 1 pound linguine
- Parmesan cheese (grated, to garnish)

HHHHHHHHHHHHHHHHHHHHHHHHHHHHHHHHH

Instructions:

1. Over moderate to high heat, heat 1 tablespoon of oil in a 12" frying pan or skillet.

2. Add the minced goose breast and cook for several minutes, until browned Transfer to a bowl.

3. Add the goose liver to the pan and cook until browned for approximately 5 minutes. Transfer to the same bowl as the breast.

4. Add the remaining oil to the pan.

5. Stir in the sage, rosemary, celery, chili flakes, onion, and carrot for 8-10 minutes, until golden. Add the wine, stirring to combine. Cook until evaporated, thicken,

6. Add the canned tomatoes and season, cook for 20-25 minutes.

7. Stir in the goose breast and liver.

8. In the meantime, cook the linguine in boiling salted water until al dente. Drain, while reserving 1 cup of pasta cooking water.

9. Add the pasta to the goose and sauce mixture, along with the reserved water. Stir gently to incorporate.

10. Garnish with cheese and enjoy.

Chapter IV - Meat-Free

HHHHHHHHHHHHHHHHHHHHHHHHHHHHHHHH

Recipe 31: Super Cheesy Linguine

Bring on the cheese. If you are a fan of cheese, then you will love this ooey-gooey cheesy linguine for two.

Yield: 2

Preparation Time: 15mins

Ingredient List:

- 7 ounces linguine
- 2 tablespoons butter
- 3 tablespoons flour
- ¼ teaspoons sea salt
- ⅛ teaspoons black pepper
- 1½ cups whole milk
- ¾ cup mozzarella cheese (shredded)
- ¼ cup Parmesan cheese (shredded)
- 2 tablespoons freshly squeezed lemon juice

HHHHHHHHHHHHHHHHHHHHHHHHHHHHHHHHH

Instructions:

1. Cook the linguine, according to the package instructions, until al dente.

2. In the meantime, in a pan over low heat, melt the butter.

3. Add the flour, sea salt, and black pepper and stir to combine.

4. Gradually, pour in the milk and bring to boil, boiling for a couple of minutes, until thickened.

5. Remove the pan from the heat.

6. In a bowl, combine the mozzarella with the Parmesan and toss with the fresh lemon juice.

7. Add the mixture to the sauce, stirring until the cheese entirely melts.

8. Drain the pasta, add the cheese sauce and toss to coat evenly.

Recipe 32: Creamy Cajun Linguine

Has your linguine got the blues? This Cajun seasoning will give this pasta dish lots of spice. It has a subtle heat and can jazz-up lots of different recipes.

Yield: 2

Preparation Time: 25mins

Ingredient List:

- 5 ounces linguine
- 2 tablespoons butter
- 1 tablespoon shallot (minced)
- 1 tablespoon garlic (peeled, minced)
- 1 tablespoon Cajun seasoning
- ¼ cup white wine
- 1 tablespoon fresh lemon juice
- ⅓ cup heavy cream
- ⅓ cup half and half
- ¼ cup Parmesan (freshly grated)
- Freshly cracked black pepper
- Chives (chopped, to garnish)

HHHHHHHHHHHHHHHHHHHHHHHHHHHHHHHHH

Instructions:

1. Cook the pasta in boiling salted water until al dente. Drain.

2. In the meantime, prepare the sauce. Over moderate heat, in a pan, melt the butter. Add the shallot along with the garlic, and Cajun seasoning and stir for 60 seconds.

3. Pour in the white wine, and while occasionally stirring, cook for between 3-4 minutes.

4. Add the fresh lemon juice, stirring a couple of times, for 60 seconds.

5. Gradually add the heavy cream followed by the half and half, stirring slowly to combine. Cook for approximately 4-5 minutes, occasionally stirring.

6. Reduce the heat to low and continue to cook for 1-2 minutes until thickened.

7. Take the pan off the heat.

8. Add the grated Parmesan and stir to incorporate. Season with pepper, to taste.

9. Finally, stir in the cooked linguine, and toss to coat evenly.

10. Garnish with chives and serve.

Recipe 33: Ricotta Linguini

Only a few very basic ingredients needed for this party-pleasing pasta dish and by using fresh, rather than dried pasta you can speed up the cooking times quite considerably.

Yield: 6

Preparation Time: 10mins

Ingredient List:

- Salt
- 1 pound fresh linguine
- 1 garlic clove (peeled, minced)
- 1 cup part-skim ricotta cheese
- 2 teaspoons fresh basil (chopped)
- Freshly ground black pepper
- 2 tablespoons Parmesan cheese (grated)

Instructions:

1. In a pan of salted boiling water cook the fresh pasta until al dente. This will take between 1-3 minutes. Drain and set 2 tablespoons of pasta cooking water to one side.

2. Add the garlic along with the ricotta cheese, and basil to a pan over medium to low heat; and cook while stirring for approximately 3-5 minutes until heated through.

3. Season to taste and add the cooked linguine along with the reserved pasta cooking water.

4. Garnish with grated Parmesan and enjoy.

Recipe 34: Greek-Style Linguine

It's time to go Greek, with this mushroom, olive, and feta pasta dish. You'll also have plenty of homemade Greek seasoning leftover to add Mediterranean flavor to future meals.

Yield: 4

Preparation Time: 8mins

Ingredient List:

Greek Seasoning:

- 1½ tablespoons dried oregano
- 1½ teaspoons salt
- 1 tablespoon onion powder
- 1½ tablespoons garlic powder
- 2 teaspoons freshly ground black pepper
- 2 teaspoons beef bouillon powder
- 2 teaspoons dried parsley flakes
- 1 teaspoon dried thyme
- 1½ tablespoons sweet paprika powder
- ¼ teaspoons ground cinnamon
- ¼ teaspoons ground nutmeg

Pasta:

- 12 ounces fresh linguine
- ¼ cup olive oil
- 4 large Portobello mushroom caps (cut in half, thinly sliced)
- 3 cloves of garlic (peeled, minced)
- 3 plum tomatoes (chopped)
- ⅓ cup Greek Kalamata olives (pitted, halved)
- 2 teaspoons Greek seasoning*

- ¾ cup Greek feta cheese (crumbled)

Instructions:

1. To make the Greek seasoning, combine all of the ingredients (oregano, salt, onion powder, garlic powder, freshly ground black pepper, 2 teaspoons beef bouillon powder, dried parsley flakes thyme, paprika, cinnamon and nutmeg and grind to a fine powder. Store in an airtight, resealable jar, until needed.

2. Cook the fresh linguine in 4 quarts of boiling salted water for 1-3 minutes, until al dente. Drain and set to one side.

3. In the meantime, in a frying pan, heat the oil over moderate-high heat.

4. Add the mushrooms, cooking and stirring until fork tender.

5. Add the garlic and cook for an additional 60 seconds.

6. Stir in the chopped tomatoes followed by the olives and seasoning, cook while stirring for a couple of minutes.

7. Add the drained pasta to the pan and toss well to coat.

8. Serve with crumbled feta cheese.

Recipe 35: Pea and Basil Linguine

The peppery, minty and sweet taste of basil pairs perfectly with baby peas and combined with al dente linguine delivers a fresh and wholesome pasta dish.

Yield: 6

Preparation Time: 25mins

Ingredient List:

- 3 tablespoons butter (divided)
- ½ cup leek (chopped)
- 1½ cups vegetable broth (divided)
- 1 (20 ounce) pack frozen petit pois peas
- 12 ounces linguine
- 1 cup fresh basil leaves
- 1 tablespoon olive oil
- 16 ounces mushrooms (stemmed, sliced)
- 1 cloves garlic (peeled, minced)
- ¼ teaspoons sea salt
- ¼ teaspoons black pepper
- ¼ cup fresh basil (chopped)

HHHHHHHHHHHHHHHHHHHHHHHHHHHHHHHHHH

Instructions:

1. Over moderate heat, in a large pan, melt 1 tablespoon of butter.

2. Add the leek and while frequently stirring, cook for 3 minutes.

3. Add ¾ cup of the broth followed by the peas and bring to boil.

4. Partially cover the pan, turn the heat down to low and simmer for approximately 5 minutes.

5. Transfer 1½ cups of the pea mixture, along with the remaining broth to a food blender and blend until silky smooth.

6. Transfer the pea puree to a bowl. Add the remaining pea mixture to the bowl, stirring to incorporate.

7. In the meantime, in a pan of boiling salted water, cook the linguine until al dente. Drain and put to one side.

8. In a pan, over moderate-high heat, melt 2 tablespoons of butter.

9. Add the mushrooms along with the garlic and sauté until fork tender, 5-6 minutes.

10. Stir in the pea mixture, cooked linguine, sea salt, and black pepper.

11. Garnish with chopped basil.

12. Serve.

Recipe 36: Lemon, Feta, and Basil Linguine

Zesty lemon and salty feta make this an ideal summer pasta dish. What's more, it uses very few ingredients and cooks exceptionally quickly.

Yield: 4

Preparation Time: 6mins

Ingredient List:

- 1 pound fresh linguine*
- ¼ cup extra-virgin olive oil
- Grated zest and freshly squeezed juice of 1 lemon
- ⅓ cup Parmesan (freshly grated)
- A handful of fresh basil leaves
- 7 ounces Greek feta cheese (crumbled)
- 2 tablespoons toasted pine nuts

HHHHHHHHHHHHHHHHHHHHHHHHHHHHHHHHH

Instructions:

1. In a large pan of boiling salted water cook the fresh pasta for 2 minutes. Drain and leave 2 tablespoons of pasta cooking water in the pan.

2. Return the linguine to the pan.

3. Add the olive oil, lemon zest, fresh lemon juice, grated Parmesan, basil and 75 percent of the feta.

4. Toss thoroughly to combine, taste and season.

5. Garnish with any remaining feta cheese along with the pine nuts.

6. Serve.

*Cook's Note: Fresh pasta takes considerably less time to cook than the dried variety. Generally, it is al dente with 1-3 minutes.

Recipe 37: Linguine with Sun-Dried Tomatoes

Sun-dried tomatoes in oil not only have an intense flavor but also they provide vitamins C, and K plus lycopene and iron. They are the perfect complement to the taste of salty feta and nutty Parmesan.

Yield: 6

Preparation Time: 15mins

Ingredient List:

- 16 ounces linguine
- 1 (7 ounce) jar julienned sun-dried tomatoes in oil
- 6 cloves garlic (peeled, minced)
- 1 tablespoon freshly squeezed lemon juice
- ½ cup fresh parsley (minced)
- 1½ cups feta cheese (crumbled)
- 1½ cups Parmesan cheese (freshly grated)

HHHHHHHHHHHHHHHHHHHHHHHHHHHHHHHH

Instructions:

1. In a stockpot of 5-6 quart capacity, cook the linguine until al dente. Drain and reserve ½ cup pasta cooking water. Return the linguine to the stockpot.

2. In the meantime, drain the tomatoes of their oil, setting 2 tablespoons of oil to one side.

3. In a microwave-safe bowl, combine the garlic together with the reserved tomato oil and on high, microwave for 45 seconds.

4. Add the drained tomatoes and fresh lemon juice, stirring to combine.

5. Fold the tomato mixture into the pasta, toss with parsley, feta, Parmesan and sufficient pasta cooking water to just moister.

6. Serve.

Recipe 38: Ligurian Pasta Trenette

Discover how to create this delicious meat-free pasta dish from Liguria, Italy. Did you know linguine originates from Genova in Liguria?

Yield: 6

Preparation Time: 30mins

Ingredient List:

- 1 pound red new potatoes (peeled, cut into large chunks)
- 1 pound green beans (trimmed, halved)
- 1 pound linguine
- 1 cup pesto sauce
- 3 tablespoons extra virgin olive oil
- Parmesan cheese (freshly grated)

HHHHHHHHHHHHHHHHHHHHHHHHHHHHHHHHH

Instructions:

1. Add the potatoes and green beans to a pan of boiling salted water and cook until the potatoes are fork-tender, 10 minutes. Using a slotted spoon, remove the veggies from the water.

2. Return the water to boil and cook the pasta until al dente.

3. Set a cup of the pasta cooking water to one side, and drain the linguine.

4. Return the drained pasta along with the cooked veggies to the pot, set aside earlier.

5. In a bowl, combine the pesto sauce with half of the reserved pasta cooking water and 3 tablespoons of olive oil. You may wish to add additional water at this point, depending on your preferred sauce consistency.

6. Pour the sauce over the linguine and veggies, tossing to coat.

7. Garnish with grated Parmesan and serve.

Recipe 39: Linguine with Mixed Nuts and Raisins

The delicate nut-like flavor of Calimyrna figs is in total harmony with pistachios, almonds and sweet golden raisins. In fact, this pasta dish is packed full of taste and texture.

Yield: 4

Preparation Time: 30mins

Ingredient List:

- 1 pound dried linguine
- ¾ cup butter
- ⅓ cup pistachios (coarsely chopped)
- ⅓ cup almonds (coarsely chopped)
- 8 dried Calimyrna Figs (chopped)
- ¼ cup golden raisins
- Sea salt
- Freshly ground black pepper
- ½ cup Parmigiano Reggiano cheese (grated)
- Grated zest of ½ medium orange
- Chives (minced, to garnish)

HHHHHHHHHHHHHHHHHHHHHHHHHHHHHHHHHH

Instructions:

1. Cook the linguine according to the package instructions and in boiling salted water, until al dente.

2. In the meantime, in a large baking dish, melt the butter.

3. When the butter is entirely melted, stir in the pistachios, almonds, figs and golden raisins.

4. Allow the butter to bubble and lightly brown. It should emit a nutty fragrance.

5. When the butter is light brown, add the drained pasta, stirring to combine and evenly coat.

6. Taste and season accordingly.

7. Fold in 75 percent of the cheese.

8. Garnish with orange zest, minced chives, and the remaining grated cheese.

9. Serve immediately.

Recipe 40: Linguine Alla Puttanesca

All fresh ingredients in this homemade pasta dish which originates from 20th century Naples.

Yield: 2

Preparation Time: 7mins

Ingredient List:

- 6 ounces fresh linguine
- 8 ounces cherry tomatoes (chopped)
- 2 tablespoons capers (rinsed)
- ½ garlic clove (peeled, crushed)
- Small bunch flat-leaf parsley (chopped)
- 1 red chili (finely chopped)
- 12 green olives (pitted, chopped)
- Freshly squeezed juice of 1 lemon
- Olive oil

HHHHHHHHHHHHHHHHHHHHHHHHHHHHHHHHH

Instructions:

1. Cook the fresh linguine in boiling salted water until al dente, this will take between 1-3 minutes. Drain.

2. Add the tomatoes, capers, garlic, parsley, chili, olives, lemon juice and a dash of olive oil to a bowl and toss to combine.

3. Fold in the drained linguine, tossing to incorporate and serve.

About the Author

Angel Burns learned to cook when she worked in the local seafood restaurant near her home in Hyannis Port in Massachusetts as a teenager. The head chef took Angel under his wing and taught the young woman the tricks of the trade for cooking seafood. The skills she had learned at a young age helped her get accepted into Boston University's Culinary Program where she also minored in business administration.

Summers off from school meant working at the same restaurant but when Angel's mentor and friend retired as head chef, she took over after graduation and created classic and new dishes that delighted the diners. The restaurant flourished under Angel's culinary creativity and one customer developed more than an appreciation for Angel's food. Several months after taking over the position, the young woman met her future husband at work and they have been inseparable ever since. They still live in Hyannis Port with their two children and a cocker spaniel named Buddy.

Angel Burns turned her passion for cooking and her business acumen into a thriving e-book business. She has authored several successful books on cooking different types of dishes using simple ingredients for novices and experienced chefs alike. She is still head chef in Hyannis Port and says she will probably never leave!

Author's Afterthoughts

With so many books out there to choose from, I want to thank you for choosing this one and taking precious time out of your life to buy and read my work. Readers like you are the reason I take such passion in creating these books.

It is with gratitude and humility that I express how honored I am to become a part of your life and I hope that you take the same pleasure in reading this book as I did in writing it.

Can I ask one small favour? I ask that you write an honest and open review on Amazon of what you thought of the book. This will help other readers make an informed choice on whether to buy this book.

My sincerest thanks,

Angel Burns

If you want to be the first to know about news, new books, events and giveaways, subscribe to my newsletter by clicking the link below

https://angel-burns.gr8.com

or Scan QR-code

Printed in Great Britain
by Amazon